LORD, SHUT MY MOUTH

HOW TO KEEP YOUR COOL WHEN YOU FEEL LIKE PEOPLE ARE CRAZY

MEGAN WRIGHT

LORD, SHUT MY MOUTH!

HOW TO KEEP YOUR COOL WHEN YOU FEEL LIKE PEOPLE ARE CRAZY

MEGAN WRIGHT

Library of Congress Cataloging-in-Publication Data

Library of Congress Number: 2023910511
ISBN: 979-8-9878343-3-6 (ebook)
ISBN: 979-8-9878343-4-3 (paperback)
ISBN: 979-8-9878343-5-0 (print)

Published in association with Called Creatives Publishing, www.calledcreativespublishing.com

Cover design: Called Creatives Publishing
Interior design: Megan Wright

2023 – First Edition

CONTENTS

INTRODUCTION

I really wanted to title this book:"People are Stupid, But God is Still Great," but I figured it would go against the premise of this study, so I asked the Lord to shut my mouth—the anthem of my life.

In a world full of free speech, do you often find yourself bothered by what others say? When opinions differ, is your first instinct to react based on your emotions or to practice a pause and respond in the Holy Spirit? It can be so easy to get wrapped up in others' words. People can say some of the rudest, most hurtful, painful, or stupid things. And then we want to set them straight or give our opinion because we know "we're right," or we get defensive and stick up for our reputation.

This was a mountain God and I went around a lot together. Seriously, I feel like he told me to put my hiking shoes on for it because there were some rocky steps I had to climb to get over it. I had a reputation for "just telling it like it is" Then I realized that meant I was judgmental and opinionated. My feelings got hurt a lot. I had high expectations of what others "should do" - like when you hold a door open for someone, and they don't say "thank you" (Gasp!). How dare they be so rude! Or, when you text someone, and they leave you on read.Here's the thing – when we put such high expectations on people, it turns our focus away from God and to our flesh and to what we think is best. After all, what we focus on becomes the center of our attention.. Moreover, when we allow other people's words to rile us up, we can tend to forget the truth of God's word, reacting based on our opinions instead of giving grace or trying to understand the full picture.

The enemy wants to keep us chained in offense because it brings strife, discontent, anger, and self-righteousness – all things that take our focus from God. He wants us to be in a stronghold of allowing others to upset us because it leaves less room for the TRUTH of God's word. The enemy wants us to talk about those wounds with others and dwell on wounds because it stirs things up.

When people use words against us, but we focus on God's truth instead, we can experience FREEDOM from the flesh feelings of offense and make like Elsa and LET IT GO.

In this study, we'll learn to break through those offenses. We'll learn biblical techniques to process emotions and respond with the Holy Spirit instead of reacting in our flesh. We'll learn how to experience emotional freedom despite what's happening around us.

SHOW ME
THE ROOTS!

DAY 1

Romans 8:5-9

Give an example of a time you set your mind on the things of the flesh instead of things above.

_____

_____

_____

When conversing with others, do you get stuck on little things? Do you tune out because you are upset at the first thing they say? Do you find yourself crafting a response in your head while you're waiting on them to finish their sentence? When you're on social media, do you find yourself quickly debating with others? Or do you become argumentative on public posts with strangers?

The answer may be no to most of these questions, but chances are there's at least one "yes." In this social media age, our mindset is "do what makes you happy" and "you do you, boo." And while those sentiments may have good intentions, they support a sense of selfishness instead of focusing on how to be in a healthy community with others. Let's face it: Unless you go off the grid, you will interact with people for the rest of your life. So, focusing on making sure you're "number 1" in every scenario will be dangerous to your well-being. Why? Because God didn't create us to be everything on our own.

We can't live our best lives without solid relationships. And to have stable relationships, we need to root them in a solid foundation – and that's where God's word comes in.

When we start to engage with God in an eternal perspective in that PEACE he talks about Romans 8:6, we rely more on HIS spirit to respond and focus more on HIS words and less on man's word.

What would it look like to set your mind on God's word?

How could it change the way you interact with people?

When continually focused on how we are hurt or wronged, we aren't focused on what is good and brings peace. I'm not suggesting that we stuff the pain. Instead, we need to process hurt feelings with God. However, if we are often upset with people, we allow opportunities for bitterness to creep in. When we are self-focused instead of God-focused, we lose opportunities for joy. We miss opportunities to serve others, and we miss opportunities to be vessels for the Kingdom.

Our brains do this weird thing when we focus on the negative – the negative starts to become our focus. Have you ever experienced that? Maybe you expect the worst from someone because they have a history of making your eyes roll. It's not healthy to be in unhealthy relationships just for the sake of giving grace. That's not the point here. It's the opposite—we must establish and live by healthy boundaries. But we need to be careful not to just cut everyone out of our lives because they tick us off. The key to living this balance is understanding how to set our minds on the peace that the Holy Spirit brings.

Where do you need to adjust your focus from "flesh to spirit"?

_____

_____

_____

_____

_____

_____

_____

_____

_____

_____

_____

_____

_____

_____

_____

_____

_____

DAY 2

Why do you think we allow other's opinions to get us riled up easily? Usually, there is something deeper going on.

_____

_____

_____

Read Luke 7:36-50

My heart desires to be like this woman. She didn't seem to care whose house she entered or what she was interrupting – she just wanted to be at the feet of Jesus. She brought her

best and kept her eyes on Him. She didn't care about the opinions of others or the judgments that would come because of her boldness.

Whom was the Woman focused on?

_____

_____

_____

Who was the Pharisee focused on?

_____

_____

_____

What was Jesus' response?

_____

_____

_____

This passage labeled the woman as a "sinner." And that's clearly what the Pharisee saw her as. And that's what his focus was on — someone he didn't think had value, someone he didn't feel "should have" been allowed in the room. He had an opportunity to serve the King of Kings in his own house, but instead, he focused on judging someone else's worth. He got so wrapped up judging this woman that he missed his opportunity with Jesus. His pride got in the way of his priority.

Describe a time when you got so wrapped up in other people's actions that you lost focus on your own.

_____

_____

_____

When have you gotten so focused on other people's actions that you missed an opportunity to point someone to Jesus?

_____

_____

_____

Proverbs 10:4: "In his pride, the wicked man does not seek him; in all his thoughts there is no room God."

Proverbs 13:10: "Where there is strife, there is pride, but wisdom is found in those who take advice."

We can get so caught up in other people's business - what they should have done or not done - that we completely lose sight of Jesus and any opportunity to point others to him. So today, pray for opportunities to be the woman instead of the Pharisee.

DAY 3

Read Luke 10:38-42

Who was Mary focused on?

_____

_____

_____

Who was Martha focused on?

_____

_____

_____

You've probably read this story many times. When I first read this passage, I immediately started reading it in character, and when I said Martha's part, I used a super sassy tone. It's almost like you can hear her attitude. Now granted, Martha and Mary were sisters, so we might easily explain the sass away, but I think the scenario often happens, regardless of the type of relationship.

When my girls got into arguments and wanted to tattle on each other, they made sure to tattle loud enough for the other to hear it. I feel like that's what Martha was doing. She seemed to be asking a rhetorical question to Jesus because she was angry and wanted to vent and get Mary in trouble.

How did Jesus respond to Martha?

_____

_____

_____

What answer do you think Martha might have wanted to hear?

_____

_____

_____

Martha thought she was to make everything perfect for Jesus. And yes, her intentions seemed to be on track: She wanted to host Jesus well. However, a seed of bitterness quickly took root. She was jealous that her sister didn't take on any chores but instead got to sit freely in the presence of Jesus. But here's the thing: Martha could have chosen to do the same thing.

When have you had similar moments of jealousy that lead to getting upset with someone?

_____

_____

_____

Have you ever had unhealthy expectations with people that led to strife?

_____

_____

_____

We've all been here. Our intentions are good, but we lose our focus. We want things to turn out perfectly, so we jump in to try and control them. If Jesus were coming to my house, I would probably react in my flesh and call a family meeting with a list of all the chores my children, husband, and dogs would be required to finish before Jesus' arrival. And then they would be mad that it wasn't done correctly. That's real life. I get it. My jealousy of someone else's healthy choice only makes me miss out on the good stuff. The God-honoring stuff.

Journal Moment

What unrealistic expectations do you need to over-come to allow for better responses and outcomes in your relationships?

1 Corinthians 3:3 "You are still worldly. For since there is jealousy and quarreling among you, are you not worldly? Are you not acting like mere humans?"

DAY 4

Read John 4:1-26

What message is Jesus trying to share with the woman?

_____

_____

_____

What would you think if you were her?

_____

_____

_____

When Jesus brought up the subject of her husband, what was her response?

_____

_____

_____

Jesus was trying to get to her heart, and because of her past and sin, she tried to avert the conversation. Good gravy, I've been there, done that, and won a trophy for it. Anyone else?

At the beginning of my marriage, I was deeply insecure. I was still processing trauma from my first marriage and trying to cover up my fears of not being worthy of another marriage, child, or chance at normal. I continually looked to my husband to fix my issues. I thought the insecurity would go away if he affirmed me in the way I needed.

But when we look to others to be our God and fill us in ways only God can, we are severely disappointed when it doesn't work. And, of course, it never works because only Jesus can fulfill that longing and void that we have; it's how God created us. But before I understood that concept, my longing turned into anger, and I reacted to people out of bitterness.

My insecurity was the filter through which I viewed other people's opinions, comments, and judgments. And that insecurity became the root of my reactions. For years, carrying on conversations with anyone was burdened with the thought that they were judging my weight and pant size because that's how I was judging myself. And so, if someone commented on anything remotely close to someone else's size, fit, health, or lifestyle, I took it personally and thought it was directed at me. My insecurities consumed me.

When have you allowed your insecurities to impact how you react to people?

Which relationships in your life are strained because they trigger your insecurities?

_____

_____

_____

When we don't believe who we are IN Jesus and instead focus on who we aren't or what we've done in our past, we lose sight of what matters. I wonder how many conversations I've had with people that have been stifled because I was so insecure that I couldn't focus on anything else except how their words might be a cut down on what I looked like, how much I weighed, or what my pant size was. That's what my focus was and where my deepest identity crisis was.

Read John 4:28-30

How does understanding your identity in Christ change how you respond to people?

_____

_____

_____

Ecclesiastes 7:21-22: "Do not take to heart all the things that people say, lest you hear your servant cursing you. Your heart knows that many times you have cursed others."

DAY 5

In the beginning years of my marriage, trust was a recurring argument. We used to throw around the "D" word a lot (and for those healthy folks who don't know what that word is, it's DIVORCE). We would get into yelling matches, and when nothing else could be topped, we would end the arguments with threats to end the marriage.

After years of therapy, I learned this was our root issues of abandonment and rejection being triggered. We feared not being accepted or "good enough" for the marriage to be successful. And in that fear, we deflected instead of working through our issues. We would tell each other (and sometimes ourselves) that ending the relationship would be best. Of course, we didn't want that for our family, but we would go straight to defensiveness when our feelings got hurt because we feared rejection.

The turning point was when we both returned to our vows and agreed not to allow ourselves to have that "out" in arguments. No matter what, we wouldn't threaten to end the marriage when we were heated.

Do you know what else God showed me through that? I had that habit in other relationships as well. I realized I had burned many bridges because I didn't understand how my past relationships triggered that fear of abandonment. So when I saw conflict coming, I hit it head-on with my sass and just chalked it up to being a "tell it how it is" type of person. I didn't want that person to reject me, so I rejected them first.

What relationships have you ended because you feared they might not stick around if a conflict arose?

Insert one of the most used Christian responses: "Jesus will never reject you." It's true: If we declare that Christ is our Savior and Lord of our life, he will never reject us, abandon us, or walk away, even if we yell at him. Understanding why and how is the key to allowing that truth to change your heart.

Read Psalm 139

What does this passage tell us about God?

What if you started living like Jesus was everywhere with you, always? How would that change your interactions with people?

What if you truly felt his presence amid conflict or amid fears that bring on triggers? How would that change your response?

....

....

....

When we engage with God with a heavenly eternal perspective, He fills us with HIS spirit, and we focus more on HIS words and less on others' words.

When people use words against us to push us away, but we truly BELIEVE that God stands firm within us, we can experience FREEDOM from the feelings of being hurt and find peace in his presence.

Journal Moment

What fears do you have that might be leading to challenges in relationships?

....

....

....

....

....

....

....

....

....

PERSPECTIVE: CHECK YOURSELF BEFORE YOU WRECK YOURSELF

DAY 1

Have you ever played the game "Telephone" with a large group of women? You're all in a circle. One person begins whispering a complete sentence to the person beside them, and then everyone spreads that same sentence to the next person until it goes around the entire circle.

I've never played the game, but typically, something like "I love my neighbor, and "I talk to her daily on the phone" turns into something like "I heard the woman at church had three kids with someone she met online." Yes, that's slightly exaggerated, but not by much. And the most obvious answer is that we hear different things when there are other background noises and pronunciations (like the women with the adorable southern draw saying things like PEE-Can versus puh-CON). But I think it's more than that. It's perspective.

Most conversations may be narrow in focus, but our outside perspectives widely influence them. Our experiences often create the lens through which we view situations. For example, I've had nasty run-ins with cats and their smells. I am a huge dog fan (I currently have seven) and pretty much any other animal fan except for cats.

When we moved into our farmhouse a few years ago, the smell was beyond words. Beyond words like when you're so disgusted, no words come to mind. We spent thousands of dollars on repairs because of the cats. This further sealed the coffin of disdain for cats in my heart. Ironically, we have several outside cats now because when you live on a farm, you either have cats or lots of mice, rats, and snakes around the house. However, the cats are not allowed to EVER come in the house. Ever. Because I am so jaded by the trauma of repairs when we first moved in, I will do whatever it takes never to have that smell in my house again.

Similarly, we can easily view relationships through jaded lenses of past pain or hurt with people. Sometimes we put up walls and do not allow people to help us because we've been hurt in the past when we've been vulnerable. Sometimes it's pulling away from people because we fear they won't accept us. Sometimes it's pushing people away because we don't want to get hurt again because somewhere along the way, our perspective shifts from our relationship wounds, and we view other relationships through those wounds.

How have past wounds caused you to change your perspective about a relationship?

_____

_____

_____

What circumstances have caused you feel jaded?

_____

_____

_____

Even though we often feel it might be easier to live alone on a deserted island, God didn't create us for that. Some studies show that our brains and bodies flourish in a close community. In fact, when God created man, he said, "It is not good for man to be alone." (Genesis 2:18)

Where do you need God to give you a fresh perspective in your relationships?

_____

_____

_____

_____

_____

_____

_____

_____

_____

_____

_____

_____

_____

_____

_____

_____

_____

_____

_____

_____

_____

DAY 2

Read John 8: 1-11

Instead of focusing on the teaching of Christ, what were the Pharisees and Scribes focused on?

....

....

....

How did Jesus respond to their accusations?

....

....

....

What happened when Jesus called them out and told them to confess their sin?

....

....

....

Gosh, it's so easy to point out others' failings or when they're doing things that we would do differently. We like to deflect or point out something in others because that takes the focus from us and where we lack because of the pride in some of us that swells up and distracts us from God.

We get so focused on other people's business that we would miss Jesus if he stood right in front of us with a big ole' name tag on.

One of the best lines I've ever heard is from a sermon years ago. The pastor said, "If you're blaming, you ain't changing." Blame shuts down opportunities for growth, connection, or reconciliation. Satan loves blame because it divides instead of unites.

Reread John 8:9-11.

After everyone had scattered, what did Jesus ask the woman?

After he imparted grace on her, what was his instruction in verse 11?

Jesus didn't disagree with the Pharisees when they said she broke the law; in fact, he told her to leave her life of sin. But it sounds like the point he was making was that they were so busy being judgmental and self-righteous that they needed a mirror moment. You know, those moments where you need to take a long look at yourself first. I wouldn't say I like mirror moments. But I'm so grateful that Jesus gently gives them to me in all his grace.

What is the Holy Spirit trying to teach that you might miss because you're too busy focusing on other people's business?

_____

_____

_____

When have you experienced a mirror moment?

_____

_____

_____

How can we be intentional about not becoming like the Pharisees?

_____

_____

_____

DAY 3

Read: 2 Corinthians 10:3-4

Draw a picture of a large fortress.

Write the root issues we identified in Week 1 in your fortress.

Fortresses were built to keep enemies out. They were built with thick materials to endure attacks and keep the people inside safe.

The term used in 2 Corinthians 10:4 for a stronghold refers to our ways of thinking.

Our root issues are our strongholds – our fortresses. They keep other people out and us secluded. They keep us alone with our issues, thoughts, and feelings. And some of us have even built motes with alligators around our fortresses for good measure.

If we don't allow others in, we lose out on healthy, life-giving relationships. And if we don't step out of our fortresses (our strongholds), we lose sight of other people's perspectives and miss out on loving as Jesus calls us to love. We can't love well when we spend all our time alone in our fortress.

How does this analogy help us to see what a stronghold is in our life?

_____

_____

_____

What feelings do you experience when you are entrapped in your fortresses?

_____

_____

_____

> Galatians 5:1 says, "It was for freedom that Christ set us free; therefore, keep standing firm and do not be subject again to a yoke of slavery."

Jesus came to give you freedom, including freedom from your fortresses!

To break through being offended, irritated, agitated, and bothered by others, we need to understand how to break free from the fortresses that keep us focused on our perspectives and allow God to give us opportunities to see from HIS perspective.

Where do you need a shift in perspective to experience the freedom that Christ offers us?

DAY 4

Read Romans 8:5-9

What does it mean to set your mind on things of the "flesh"?

....

....

....

When we constantly think of ourselves and how things affect us, we become blind to the bigger picture. When our problems, woes, pains, aggravations, and annoyances are things we stew over, they get in the way of seeing everything else. This scripture says that when we focus on the "flesh," it's death. And I've noticed that when I'm constantly focused on my perspective, my heart isn't open to what others are going through because what we focus on becomes our focus.

What are some examples of "flesh" things that we can easily get too focused on?

....

....

....

How does verse 6 describe a mind "set on the spirit"?

_____

_____

_____

Life and Peace. We are void of peace when we focus so much on things, jobs, problems, and grievances with others. And our hearts know that because of the tension we feel amid those things. But when we invite Christ into the picture and ask for his perspective, his peace that transcends all understanding seems to flood our hearts, and none of those annoyances seem to be a big deal anymore.

What does verse 7-8 say happens when we focus on the flesh?

_____

_____

_____

How can we possibly please God if pleasing God isn't our focus?

_____

_____

_____

Christ-followers don't have an easier way in life than non-believers. We don't just wake up and float through life because we call Jesus our Savior. Unfortunately, it's just as easy for us to follow the latest social media hashtag, the fear-instilling news channels, and the "you do you boo" mantras.

But we have hope, the living word, and prayer. And those things change the world when we trust them.

When someone ticks us off, we can choose how we receive, react, and respond. It's the difference between staying in our flesh (self-centered thoughts, grievances, anger) or bringing Spirit-filled life through our responses.

Read Romans 8:10-11

When we ask God to come into our thoughts and conversations, it allows space for him to move in ways that we never could.

How have you lost focus on the things that matter for eternity because you're stuck on things of the flesh?

What areas of your life do you need a focus adjustment in?

Ask God to reveal where you need to focus more on the eternal perspective (what matters for the Kingdom of God) and what things you need to let go of to do so.

DAY 5

Read Luke 6:27-36

What does this passage say about crazy people (as scripture calls them "enemies")?

_____

_____

_____

What does verse 35 say about what we should expect in return?

_____

_____

_____

Whom do we have as an example according to verses 35-36?

_____

_____

_____

When I gave birth to my youngest, I had a C-section and my tubes tied at the same time. I worked remotely and returned to work about two weeks after those surgeries. Two months later, I was back in the hospital, having emergency surgery to remove my gallbladder. About six months later, I had three discs herniate at the same time, so I went back into the outpatient surgery room. It was the same year the market crashed. so my husband and I lost our jobs. We went from a six-figure income to $260 a week from unemployment benefits and food stamps. You can imagine the stress in our household – well, it was about ten times worse than that. I think everything erupted inside when I was holding my infant, and my husband was doing the dishes and asked if I would please not put dishes in the sink with food still on them.

I lost it. And I wanted to punch my husband in Jesus' name. But, instead, I went and had a good cry in the shower. I was praying, dropped to my knees in despair, and as I looked down, I saw the word FAITH written on my hand with my veins. It was one of those "seeing Jesus in a grilled cheese sandwich" moments.

I had gotten so stressed out from all the things. I was tired. I had lost hope. And I came undone because of a comment about dishes. I was allowing my circumstance to swallow me, and I could not see outside it. What I realized was that I wasn't trusting God. I wasn't trusting God with circumstances or my heart.

Our perspectives can dictate how we view and receive people's comments, opinions, or reactions.

And because I wasn't trusting God with my heart, everything hurt: Every word, every look, every unspoken thing I would make up from assumptions instead of facts because I was struggling.

And that's what I have realized about people acting crazy: They are often the ones that are struggling the most, having let their emotions get the best of them. And sometimes, that comes out in pride, insecurity, and fear or through nasty comments or actions. Hurt people, hurt people, right?

How are you allowing circumstances to dictate your reactions?

_____

_____

_____

What moments have you had where small things caused big problems?

_____

_____

_____

When have you been on the receiving end of hurt from hurting people?e

_____

_____

_____

What would happen if you trusted that God would take care of your heart from those wounds and opted for forgiveness and release as your response?

God, may we be women who have ears to hear!

Exodus 14:14: "The LORD will fight for you, and you have only to be silent."

THE POWER OF THE TONGUE

DAY 1

I remember the first time I tried to ride my hot-tempered horse without a bit. I remember it well because I haven't done it since. We'd trained together for several months. I knew she trusted me more than she had ever trusted anyone, so I thought it would be a turning point for us - like one of those moments in movies where the bond between animal and human is undeniable and life-changing. I mounted her bareback and slowly began walking off. At first, it was this liberating sense of accomplishment. I was amazed that I was riding her without a saddle or bit and was gaining confidence with every step. Then, my leg rubbed her side and spooked her, and she quickly sidestepped. Without a bit in her mouth to calm her down and regain control, I promptly face-planted on the hard ground beside her.

Several other times in our training have gone rodeo, bucking bronco style, trying to buck me off. But with a bit in her mouth, I can redirect her focus and get her back on track. I can guide her, keep her trust, and build a beautiful bond for both of us.

Read James 3:3-5

This analogy that James uses in 3:3 hits home for me.

How does verse 3 explain what a bit is for?

How is that like our tongue (verse 5)?

Our tongue is this tiny little thing that holds incredible power. When it's out of control, and we don't use it properly, it can cause immense pain to ourselves and others. But when we use it with self-control, we can guide, teach, heal, build trust, and encourage in a beautifully fulfilling way.

Our words bring life or death.

Proverbs 12:13: "An evil man is trapped by his rebellious speech, but a righteous man escapes from trouble."

When do you struggle with controlling your mouth?

Are there certain people or situations that trigger comments from you that might wound or cause pain (to you or others)?

What potential root causes of those triggers might be bringing out hurtful words (i.e., insecurity, control, pride, fear)?

Proverbs 21:23: "He who guards his mouth, keeps his soul from distress."

DAY 2

I think everyone can remember being told words that have left wounds - that, in many cases, have been things we've held on to or things we've allowed to change our self-esteem, identity, and confidence.

What words have been said *to* you that have had a negative impact on your life?

How did those words change your perspective?

How did they prevent you from doing something God called you to do?

_____

_____

_____

What words have been said _to_ you that positively impacted your life?

_____

_____

_____

How did they offer encouragement?

_____

_____

_____

The more weight we put into words, the heavier the burden of our self-worth becomes. So as we mature spiritually, we learn to separate people's words from our identity.

The more you know about what God wants you to focus on, the less time you have to focus on yourself and your flaws. Likewise, the more you understand God's perspective, the less you focus on a self-perspective.

What does Matthew 16:24 say about our focus on ourselves?

_____

_____

_____

When we are in the Word and longing to know more about Him, our perspective shifts from us to Him. Through the Word, we find our identity in HIM, not in what we have been told or feel!

Romans 6:6: For we know that our old self was crucified with him so that the body ruled by sin might be DONE AWAY WITH, that we should no longer be SLAVES to sin (or feelings or other's words!)

1 Peter 2:9 "But you are a CHOSEN people, a ROYAL priesthood, a HOLY nation, God's SPECIAL POSSESSION, that you may declare the praises of him who called you out darkness into his wonderful light."

Do you act like royalty?

Do you truly believe that YOU ARE GODS SPECIAL POSSESSION?

Does your heart rest knowing that YOU ARE CHO-SEN by GOD?

Write 1 Peter 2:9.

Now write these statements: I am CHOSEN. I am royalty. I am God's special possession.

Share with God why you struggle to believe these truths.

Where has your identity been rooted in your life?

My identity's roots have been different in different seasons. It was rooted in my weight and pant size for many seasons. For other seasons, it was rooted in my career.

When we believe and trust our identity in Jesus, we experience freedom from the weight of others' words.

_____

_____

_____

When you know the truth of the Bible, you are equipped to overcome the words that have scarred you, wounded you, and jaded your perspective.

_____

_____

_____

DAY 3

Read James 3:6-12

What is this passage saying about our "tongues"?

_____

_____

_____

How does the analogy of a flame relate to our words?

_____

_____

_____

Write down a time when you used words that didn't build someone up.

_____

_____

_____

Write down a time when you know you made a difference with your words.

_____

_____

_____

Both are powerful examples of how we can influence others with our words. How we use our words and how we are affected by others' words – both shift with a Godly perspective.

How we process and react to words from others will change the more we align our perspectives and hearts with the word of GOD. How we use OUR words can deliver God's freedom over others.

_____

_____

_____

Proverbs 18:21: "The tongue has the power of life and death, and those who love it will eat its fruit."

What do you think this scripture means?

_____

_____

_____

Whatever you're putting out there will draw people in. You get to decide what you draw them in with. Do you want to spread life and foster further life-giving, encouraging words? Or will you choose to spread words that don't build others up? This scripture says that when we do that, we'll be surrounded by negative

conversations and negative people because it's those kinds of people that we draw in. Negativity breeds negativity, just as encouragement breeds encouragement.

DAY 4

Read Proverbs 2: 1-12 and circle the word wisdom

Reread Verse 12.

What does wisdom deliver us from?

My old horse trainer once said, "The end of knowledge is the beginning of frustration." That changed my perspective on training my horse, but it is even more applicable to people. It's like that cliché saying, "hurt people, hurt people." Of course, it doesn't make it right, and it's not an excuse for their bad behavior, but it allows us to look at the bigger picture and seek wisdom to impart peace instead of sassiness.

When you're in emotionally painful situations, do your words reflect that?

When we don't understand someone else's pains and perspectives, we assume the worst and take things personally. But when we seek wisdom, we're asking God for an understanding of things we don't get.

When people are rude, do you ever stop and ask God for a different perspective?

How might this help in your reactions?

Proverbs 10:19 "When words are many, sin is unavoidable, but he who restrains his lips is wise."

Ecclesiastes 10:12 "Words from the mouth of a wise man are gracious, while the lips of a fool consume him;"

God must have really wanted us to understand this point - our mouths are our most powerful weapon, and how we choose to fight will determine what we want our victories to be.

Read Ephesians 5:15-21

When I am careful how I live out my walk through my words and focus on the truth of God's word, I can more easily spread the goodness of it to others! When we seek God first for wisdom — for HIS WISDOM- our perspective starts to change over words. Words that once might have broken us no longer have power over us because we know the TRUTH. Words we once might have used to defend, block, or intentionally hurt others won't be unfiltered because we aren't reactionary; instead, we seek wisdom to deliver us.

DAY 5

A few years back, my two daughters and I were boarding a plane headed back home from an amazing Disney World trip. I couldn't sit next to them, so I had them sit together. I was seated in the row in front of them. This made way for an unfortunate encounter that I'm now using as an excellent example for the entire premise of this book.

The girls had to sit next to a grumpy older man. He had the aisle seat. His wife was seated across from him (looking back, she might have done that on purpose). The plane had just taken off. The man was very hungry (some might say hangry) and ready to get after his sub sandwich. Well, my timid daughter had to pee, so with her best manners, she asked to get up, to which the grumpy old man with absolutely no manners replied with a nasty "no" and then questioned why she couldn't wait until he was finished eating, amongst other nasty comments.

Overhearing this all, with all kinds of Momma Bear rage, I calmly turned around and told him because she was a child and not able to hold it that long. He was surprised to realize that her mother was there to defend her. What I know about that moment is that it was a great opportunity for my daughters to see how to keep their cool when others are crazy.

Even when we have a cause, we still pause.

Even when we have a legitimate cause to be upset or offended, we pause and say, "LORD, SHUT MY MOUTH." We process it; we look from the other person's perspective. Then, we make like Elsa and let it go. We smother it with GRACE like the south does with gravy over biscuits, and we respond with gentleness instead of reacting from our feelings.

When do find yourself often reacting from your feelings if people do things that bother you?

....

....

....

....

....

....

Are there areas in your life where you need to practice the pause?

....

....

....

....

....

Proverbs 19:11 "Good sense makes one SLOW to anger,
and it is his glory to overlook an offense."

James 1:19: "But everyone must be quick to hear, slow to
speak, and slow to anger."

When we start to practice the pause and ask God for his wisdom to respond, we shift our perspective from us to Him.

_____

_____

_____

Journal Moment

Ask God to reveal where you need help practicing the pause. And in that pause, ask for God's perspective, wisdom, and revelation for a fresh perspective on how your response can bring life instead of death.

_____

_____

_____

_____

_____

_____

_____

_____

_____

_____

_____

_____

_____

_____

_____

TOTAL ECLIPSE OF THE HEART

DAY 1

Matthew: 12:34 For out of the OVERFLOW of the heart, the mouth speaks.

Proverbs 4:23: Keep your heart with all vigilance, for from it flow the springs of life.

Where do these scriptures say that our Words come from?

_____

_____

_____

Luke 6:45: "The good person out of the good treasure of the heart produces good, and the evil person out of evil treasure produces evil; for it is out of the abundance of the heart that the mouth speaks."

Something is typically happening in our hearts when our words are hurtful, curt, or snide.

I see folks searching for advice from so many different avenues, and my first question is always: Have you prayed on it? It always brings up a question: How long would it take to miss him if the Holy Spirit were gone? People long for confirmation and acceptance from others so much that they forget to ask Jesus first when they need confirmation.

Isaiah 9:6 says that Jesus is our wonderful counselor, Mighty God, Eternal Father, and Prince of Peace.

God surrounds us with people to help, encourage, spur, and point us to His Word. But that's the key – we need the Word to nurture our hearts.

We need the Word to guide, counsel, grow, and encourage us with peace. It's the FIRST place that we should always go to.

_____

_____

_____

Proverbs 23:7: "As a man thinks, so is he."

Whatever we have going on in our hearts that is unresolved, that's where our words will come from! If there is unresolved anger, jealousy, or hurt, it will simmer into bitterness in the heart. And I mean simmer because those things can sit for a while and go unchecked on a low bubble until it's gone on for so long that it's burning because it's festered so hot inside.

What is unresolved in your heart right now?

_____

_____

_____

_____

_____

_____

How has it caused bitterness toward anyone?

_____

_____

_____

_____

_____

Get to the heart of it to guard your tongue.

_____

_____

_____

_____

_____

_____

DAY 2

Israel had not heard from God in decades. The priests were corrupt. The nearby nations threatened the land's safety. Even Eli, Israel's high priest and judge, did not faithfully serve God and the people. So, God gives them <u>Samuel</u>. Samuel served the people as a prophet and judge. He taught them how to live as the people of God. But the people were determined to have a king, so they eventually demanded Samuel appoint one; God gave them Saul. Saul was an idiot. Scripture says he is a foolish, selfish, and cowardly King. He ignored the word of the Lord and craved the approval of men. He disobeyed God several times and put the people at odds with God and each other. King Saul did not keep the Law of Moses nor direct the Israelites to live as God's holy people.

Read 1 Samuel 16

In this chapter, God instructs Samuel to appoint another King. But he clues him on how to do it.

Reread 1 Samuel 16:7.

What does God say that he looks at first?

....

....

....

Our words soon follow when our hearts don't align with God. And our words then dictate our actions. There are a lot of "Sauls" out there, and God's seeking leaders by looking at their hearts.

Read Psalm 139: 24-25

Have you ever asked God to search your heart?

....
....
....

Journal Moment

Pray Psalm 139: 24–25 and write what God is stirring in your heart.

....
....
....
....
....
....
....
....
....
....

May we be bold women asking God to lead us in the everlasting way.

DAY 3

Romans 8:5: For those who live according to the flesh set their minds on the things of the flesh, but those who live according to the Spirit set their minds on the things of the Spirit.

What are examples of things of the spirit?

_____

_____

_____

What are examples of things of the flesh?

_____

_____

_____

When my younger daughter, Savannah, was little, she had moments where she would get caught up in thinking about bad things happening to me, which would physically cause her angst. She would cry and work herself up; it was the saddest thing! I would remind her that thinking about "what ifs" never brought anything good.

When do you struggle with "what if's"?

_____

_____

_____

What are some typical "what if's" that you stress over?

_____

_____

_____

How are those working for you? But for real – I wonder how much time we waste thinking about things out of our control. And what we could have been doing instead was fruitful.

Read 2 Corinthians 10:3-5

When I get to heaven, I'm going to ask God why I always have so many RANDOM thoughts that pop into my head. Until then, we have to equip ourselves with God's Word. We must fight to keep our thoughts in check, but God gives us the weapons to do so: His word, people, and peace. We CHOOSE what happens to those thoughts and how far we let them get out of control.

What thoughts are you consistently struggling with right now?

_____

_____

_____

How would you experience freedom if you learned how to stop them?

....

....

....

"You cannot keep birds from flying over your head, but you
can keep them from building a nest in your hair."
Martin Luther

DAY 4

Have you ever had a dream so real that when you woke up, you were angry with the people in it? Maybe it's a dream where your spouse cheats on you with your best friend. Those are the worst. The first time I had a dream like this, I was so angry with Tom that I marched right to him and told him every detail and how mad I was! I'm sure he felt like that was a trap.

Or do you play out extensive conversations in your head with people? You rehearse every possible scenario of how the talk could go, and then you get heated over something that is just in your head.

When someone is sassy with you or says something rude, do you often think about it over and over in your head?

_____

_____

_____

God's created people who have built rocket ships that send us to the moon. He's created people that developed technology, allowing us to talk to anyone, anywhere in the world, at any time. Just think about all the discoveries and inventions we've seen over the last 20 years. It's crazy. And our brains create, imagine, and build all of it. So our minds are POW-ERFUL things.

And how we use our brains will determine how we live. What we focus on becomes our focus. It's like the crabby people known for negativity are often the most miserable because negativity festers and builds, becoming their world.

Have you ever known people like that?

Read Romans 12:2

_____

_____

_____

What does this verse instruct us to do?

_____

_____

_____

How can we renew our minds?

_____

_____

_____

Reading God's word, connecting with his church, praying – all these things renew our minds!

What does this verse say that renewing our minds does?

_____

_____

_____

Are there thought patterns that rob your peace?

_____

_____

_____

Journal Moment

Ask God what thoughts you need to release to renew your mind.

_____

_____

_____

_____

_____

_____

_____

_____

_____

_____

Philippians 4:9: "Finally, brothers and sisters, whatever is true, whatever ever is noble, whatever is right, whatever is pure, whatever is lovely, whatever is admirable – if anything is excellent or praiseworthy – think about such things."

What praiseworthy things in your life can you think about to foster a positive perspective?

DAY 5

Stop the thoughts. Confess those thoughts to God. Speak truth into existence (His WORD).

You get to choose how someone's words affect you. If it hurts, you can choose to process it in prayer and petition in God's word, or you can choose to hold on to it, allowing resentment, bitterness, and anger to creep in. Unfortunately, that's usually when our hearts are ripe for being offended.

1 Corinthians 14:26: "What then, brothers? When you come together, each one has a hymn, a lesson, a revelation, a tongue, or an interpretation. Let all things be done for building up."

If we are focused on doing everything to build up, God will use that to transform our thoughts to align with his!

Where are you tearing down instead of building up?

When you engage in conversations with crazy people, what would happen if you had the motive of building up?

_____

_____

_____

Several years ago, wearing hats, shirts, and jewelry with the saying "follow your heart" was trendy. I get the sentiment in theory, but that perspective has led to many unhealthy toxic relationships. Because when our hearts are wounded, bitter, lost, indecisive, or based on circumstances, they can lead us down selfish rabbit holes.

Jeremiah 17:9 "The heart is deceitful above all things, and desperately sick; who can understand it?"

Have you ever met a teenage girl in "love"? Shoot, I was one many times, and if I'd have followed my heart in every one of those scenarios…well, let's not go there. But I think you might understand.

Don't follow your heart – follow God's.

GREAT EXPECTATIONS, OPINIONS, AND JUDGMENTS – OH MY!

DAY 1

You probably know someone who is a "should have" type of person, sharing their opinions on everything wrong with everyone and everything around them. I think we all tend to be this person. I definitely used to be this person.

It's like when you hold the door for someone still a bit far away, and you're waiting and waiting, and they finally walk through, but then they don't say thank you. And you want to turn your neck in a quick, snappy way and yell after them in a loud voice, "YOU'RE WELCOME."

Or have you ever helped someone repeatedly, and then when you were in a position of need, you asked them for their help, and they turned you down? The typical reaction might be to quickly recall all the ways that you've been there for them, right?

Read Romans chapter 14

What is this passage talking about?

What are all the commandments listed in this chapter (write them down)?

....

....

....

....

What are his reasons for all the commandments (write them down)?

....

....

....

How do all these things relate to unhealthy expectations?

....

....

....

> *Verse 12 sounds like Paul is saying, "you worry about*
> *yourself and let God focus on everyone else."*

Expectations lead to disappointment, resentment, anger, and distrust. Sisters, we are called to do what leads to peace and building each other up. If we get wrapped up in the little things that mean nothing to the Kingdom of Heaven, we miss out on exactly that – the Kingdom of Heaven right here on earth.

Do you have people in your life that hold you to unhealthy expectations?

_____

_____

_____

What is a common expectation that you have for people?

_____

_____

_____

Have you ever had a severed relationship because of unmet expectations?

_____

_____

_____

Ask God if there are unhealthy expectations that you need to release to allow for more peace in your life.

DAY 2

Read Matthew 25 1-13

How were these women described?

_____

_____

_____

What did the "foolish" women expect the "prudent" women to do?

_____

_____

_____

These fools (that's not my opinion, it's literally how the passage describes them) weren't responsible enough to prepare. So when the most important time came in their lives, they expected the people who had prepared to step in, sacrifice their preparation, and help.

What did the foolish women miss out on?

When we put our expectations onto others, we will miss encounters with Jesus because we are too focused on how we've been wronged or how someone "should have" done something for us.

Have you ever had a "foolish moment" and expected someone to fix the problem without considering their situation?

Have you ever been the "prudent" one in situations?

Or what about when you haven't been able to help someone and then react from a bitter place, bringing up past situations where they have been the one who has helped you?

Sometimes people tie their good deeds to expectations of getting something in return. That's probably where the saying "no strings attached" originated.

We think we are the rule makers on how people should act, and then when they don't follow those rules, we get our undergarments in a bunch and become angry and aggravated. All while yelling, "Be kind!" to them as we roll our eyes and stomp off the other way.

The parable Jesus teaches in Matthew 25 is about the Kingdom of Heaven and being prepared. It offers a great example of how we can miss Jesus if we expect or assume too much from others.

Are there areas where you've let unhealthy expectations get in the way of spiritual growth and peace?

Ask God where you might have unhealthy expectations of people or relationships.

DAY 3

Matthew 15 1-20

What did the Pharisees and Scribes ask Jesus in verse 2?

These guys walked all the way from Jerusalem to ask why the disciples weren't following their "traditions." Jesus spoke to the heart of the Pharisees; they were focused on their expectations of how things "should" be done, and they missed the opportunity to have real authenticity with the King of Kings.

What did Jesus call them in verse 7?

Why do you think he called them that?

Then Jesus commands a crowd to gather around to bring the point home.

What do you think verse 11 means?

....

....

....

This goes back to what we studied last week – the root issues in the heart. Based on the Pharisees' question, Jesus knew what their heart was full of. Out of the overflow of the heart, the mouth speaks.

What does verse 12 say happened?

....

....

....

Are we shocked that they got offended?

....

....

....

I love verse 14; read it again.

When I read this verse, I think of two crabby old women, smoking and drinking scotch while sitting on the phone gossiping with the neighbor about a mutual "friend" and going on for hours about their disgust and disdain. I might have this vision because I have a faint memory of a distant family member doing this when I was a kid (she's passed on, so there's no way she can read this book and be offended). I do know one thing for sure – there's not much fullness of joy in people that make it a habit of stirring drama up.

The devil wants you to be upset and then find someone to talk about being upset with because it distracts from Jesus.

Write about a time that you were so focused on expectations (the "should haves" or "would haves") that you lost focus on following Jesus.

_____

_____

_____

_____

_____

_____

_____

_____

Where in your life do you need to release expectations and ask God for his perspective?

_____

_____

_____

_____

_____

_____

_____

_____

_____

May we boldly ask God to uproot the plants he hasn't planted in our hearts.

DAY 4

Years ago, I had a good friend going through an extremely challenging time in her marriage. For about a year, I was the one she called every day. She cried, she vented, we prayed, and she asked my advice. She was lonely and frustrated and wanted things to be different. I would cry out to God on her behalf. But nothing ever changed. And it wasn't because God didn't step in; it was because she never did anything different.

I noticed I was starting to get upset about this situation. I started venting to my husband about her situation and how I had given so much advice, yet nothing changed. Something shifted. I had become bitter and frustrated with her because she wasn't taking hold of her situation and doing what we had discussed so many times. I had become short-tempered in our conversations and wanted to go over to her house and give her and her husband a piece of my mind.

My desire to be a good friend to her had an underlying root of control tied to it. I truly wanted to help her. I saw a very clear way to solve her issue. I was giving her advice and expecting her to take it. And because she didn't, I was angry with her. And that anger caused tension in our friendship, but it also caused tension in my marriage and my personal walk with God. I realized that to have a healthy relationship, I had to set some boundaries around what we could talk about together and what things we needed to stay clear of – her marriage was one of those things.

Scripture is clear that we are to share its wisdom, spur others towards it, sharpen with it, and use it to help people grow. But we are not God.

When have you shared repeated advice with someone that didn't act on it?

....

....

....

How did that cause tension in the relationship?

....

....

....

Do you ever find yourself giving advice but getting upset when people don't take it? Why do you think it bothers you?

....

....

....

In 1 Kings, we read about King Solomon and his 40-year reign that brought Israel peace, wealth, and prosperity. 1 Kings 10:23 says that he became greater than all the kings of the earth and had wisdom that God put in his heart. When he died, his son Rehoboam took the throne.

Read 1 Kings 12 1-7

When Rehoboam faced his first challenge as king, what did he do?

_____

_____

_____

When he sought advice from the wise counsel, what did they say would happen if he listened to them?

_____

_____

_____

Read verse 8.

What did Rehoboam do?

_____

_____

_____

Read 1 Kings 12:19

This passage tells us that Rehoboam faced extreme consequences when he did not take the advice of the wise people God had put in his life. Many people suffered because of his decision, but God allowed him to make that decision.

Read 1 Corinthians 6-9

According to this passage, what are we responsible for?

_____

_____

_____

If we are responsible for planting the seeds of scripture, who is responsible for growing them?

_____

_____

_____

How does this relate to giving advice?

_____

_____

_____

Be the person that plants the seeds. Offer biblical advice. Point people to the Word. But let God do the rest.

DAY 5

Ultimately, the core root of expectations is CONTROL. We desire to control things, circumstances, and, most of all, people. We want to be allowed to say what we want when we want, but we don't want that for others because we can't control it. Oh, the tangled webs we weave.

Read Romans 2: 1-11

What are verses 1-3 talking about?

_____

_____

_____

How are judgment and control related?

_____

_____

_____

What leads us to repentance, according to verse 4?

_____

_____

_____

One time Tom and I fought, and I was so upset that I locked myself in the bathroom and cried out to God. He answered quickly and reminded me that he loved Tom with as much forgiveness as he loved me. I didn't like that answer at the time. I wanted God to bring his Holy Spirit conviction to Tom in the most powerful, mighty way. But I knew at that moment he was growing ME; it had nothing to do with Tom.

When we choose to overlook things, we are choosing to show others the love of Christ. It's our greatest defense. When our emotions and expectations aren't tied to others, it truly brings freedom only Christ can bring.

It doesn't mean we pretend things don't hurt; we have feelings. But when we take those wounds to God first and ask for his perspective and sufficiency, he shows up in ways that only he can, taking the pain that only he can truly heal.

And you can always do what I do and turn everything into a Disney Singalong –be like Elsa and "let it go."

GRACE: SMOTHER IT LIKE BISCUITS OVER GRAVY

DAY 1

Grace isn't my spiritual gift. I feel like I've coined this phrase. I'm unsure if that's the reputation I want, but I know I'm saved and still sassy. Knowing I'm not spiritually gifted with grace doesn't give me a free ride. It doesn't give me a pass to bulldoze through people. Unfortunately, I've come to realize that for me, it means I have to work extra hard at being intentional with my grace-giving. I've been told I'm "extra" many times in my life, but that's due to the obscene amount of sequins and rhinestones in my closet, definitely not for the grace I extend.

I think we've all met those people who are gifted with extending grace. And not the fake kind of grace that lacks boundaries and allows people to treat them poorly. I'm talking about the people that have healthy relationships from wisdom and discernment, and they walk in confidence, knowing that the cross covers everyone's sins, not just their own.

I want to be that when I grow up.

Read Exodus Chapter 33.

What is Moses experiencing in this chapter?

_____

_____

_____

In his frustration, what did Moses ask God for in verses 12-13?

_____

_____

_____

What does God grant Moses in verse 17?

_____

_____

_____

What does God say he will do in verse 19?

_____

_____

_____

In the Old Testament, God's favor is grace itself. It's what he showed Moses, despite the Israelite's idolatry toward other Gods and their blatant disobedience.

> *Exodus 34:6 "Then the Lord passed in front of him (Moses) and proclaimed, 'The LORD, the LORD God, compassionate and gracious, slow to anger and abounding loving-kindness and truth.'"*

What are the characteristics of God, according to this verse?

_____

_____

_____

He's the definition of grace: compassionate, slow to anger, abounding in loving-kindness and truth.

What if we used this definition as a sort of checklist that we went through before responding to the crazy, curt, snide, or hurtful things from others? You see, it's us being intentional. It's us working at it. We take that pause and respond instead of reacting because it doesn't come naturally for most of us.

When we truly understand the magnitude of our sin and how God's grace has covered it, we have a desire that's awakened for transformation. I was once so lost in alcohol, sex, insecurity, and promiscuity, but now I'm found in the roots of scripture. That's God's grace and mercy manifested in my life. And because I've experienced that deep forgiveness and redemption, I understand the impact of grace. And I want my life to reflect that. I want people to know how grace can change your life.

How has God's grace been evident in your life?

_____

_____

_____

How have you changed since experiencing his grace?

_____

_____

_____

DAY 2

*Read these verses: Psalm 86:15, Psalm 103:8, Psalm
111:4, Psalm 112:4, Psalm 116:5, Psalm 145:8*

What is the commonality in all of these passages?

_____

_____

_____

How do these verses describe God?

_____

_____

_____

I believe with all my heart that the more something is refer-
enced in scripture, the more we need to hear it. If being full
of compassion and loving kindness was human nature, our
world wouldn't be in as much turmoil. It's quite the opposite.
The more we rely on ourselves, the more we lack what God
desires for us.

God's loving-kindness is engrained in our DNA and gen-
erational history, and yet, here we live in our modern culture
where the words "Be Kind" are being sold on t-shirts as al-

most a new concept and way of living. It's not new at all; in fact, it's almost as old as humanity. But we need that reminder because it is easy to choose the alternative.

2 Corinthians 9:8: "And God is able to make all grace abound to you, so that having all sufficiency in all things at all times, you may abound in every good work."

Who is the giver of grace?

_____

_____

_____

When do we have grace available to us?

_____

_____

_____

What are we called to do with grace?

_____

_____

_____

God gives us enough grace for ourselves and our actions. He says it's sufficient. Sufficiency means it's all we need. He then says that we can abound in good words within that sufficiency.

When people are crazy, the sufficiency of God's grace is all we need <u>SO THAT</u> we can point them to GOD because that's what is most important – the eternal perspective - the perspective that God allows us to give him glory and show others the same grace we've received. The eternal perspective shows others that despite their ridiculous actions, we as Christ imitators, can imitate grace and then press on in the good works God has for us.

Who has God placed in your life that desperately needs to experience his loving kindness and compassion?

_____

_____

_____

Those completely void of compassion, kindness, and grace often aren't good at extending it.

Where do you need to be more intentional to respond with grace?

_____

_____

_____

Ask God to reveal where you've received an abundance of his grace, write down your gratitude for his
loving kindness and then ask him where you need to
extend it to others.

DAY 3

Read 2 Corinthians 12:7-9.

What did Paul pray three times for?

_____

_____

_____

_____

_____

_____

_____

We aren't sure of the details of Paul's torment, but we know it was so extreme that he prayed to God for relief. And God's response was, "My grace is sufficient." He didn't tell Paul that he would stop the enemy's attacks for him; he didn't tell him that he would clear the way or immediately provide relief – none of that. God's response was, "My grace is sufficient."

When others come at you, his grace is sufficient. When someone doesn't act as we want them to, His grace is sufficient. When someone doesn't meet our expectations, His grace is sufficient.

Is there anyone specific in your life that comes to mind that you need to extend more grace to?

_____

_____

_____

Read Colossians 4:5-6.

What instruction does Paul give to believers?

_____

_____

_____

What should our conversations always be full of?

_____

_____

_____

We know that salt enhances flavors; it brings out the best in whatever you're cooking. It makes food come alive. Without it, things are bland and forgettable, lacking fullness and satisfaction.

Years back, I was diagnosed with mold poisoning, which led to a blood circulation disorder. This disorder causes nasty symptoms and black-out episodes. It took several doctors to get a proper diagnosis and treatment plan. One of the unique instructions from my doctor was to eat an obscene amount of salt every single day. The irony is that my husband always jokes that I'm like Kentucky Fried Chicken in my home cooking, using "11 herbs and spices." He's not wrong. My spice cabinet Is much like my clothes closet – full. My doctor said I needed as much salt as possible for my blood to circulate properly. Salt was one of the things that God used to bring a lot of healing to my body over the last few years.

So not only does salt taste good, it heals. The parallel between my physical healing journey and Colossians 4:6 is fascinating.

Salt is always available, easy to find, and abundant in quantity. And it brings life and healing, just like grace.

Ask God if your conversations are full of grace; write down areas of your life that need more salt.

DAY 4

Everyone needs GRACE just like we need GRACE; the more we extend it, the more we receive it. I can't count the times that God has been gracious to me just over the last week because it's in abundance, and I know because of that grace that he's given to me – he wants me to give it to others. No matter how much I don't want to or feel like someone doesn't deserve it. The truth is, none of us deserve as much grace as we've been given. But that's the beauty of God's gifts. They aren't things that we can earn.

And so, when we release the control of wanting to divvy out the grace based on our opinions of who deserves it and step into the righteous notion that it's our just God who gets to make those determinations, then we truly will experience the freedom that God offers through our submission to him.

Releasing control allows us to submit to the grace of God.

Read Galatians 5: 13-18.

By Christ, we are free, how are we to use that freedom, according to verse 13?

How does that relate to us communicating in relationships with others?

_____

_____

_____

Verse 15 talks about "biting and devouring each other," what are some examples of that in our society?

_____

_____

_____

What instruction does Paul give in verse 16?

_____

_____

_____

After going through this study, what would it look like for you to start walking by the Spirit?

_____

_____

_____

I was born and raised in Virginia, but I've always had most of my extended family live in the south. My great-grandma, who lived in Georgia, was known for her southern cooking and baking. And I remember her cooking biscuits and gravy often. But you could never see the biscuits because they were absolutely smothered in her gravy.

That's how we should use grace. Smother it over everything.

Read Galatians 5:22-26

This passage teaches us how to "walk by the spirit." When we focus more on love, joy, peace, patience, kindness, goodness, faithfulness, gentleness, and self-control – there's not much room for anything else.

Journal Moment

Ask God to reveal where you need more "fruit" in walking by the spirit and write down what you will start doing intentionally to grow it.

DAY 5

Are we practicing the PAUSE when someone wounds us? Are we doing a Holy Spirit check-in to keep our thoughts in check? Are we demolishing our expectations so that we can be free from being angered by others not meeting them?

Are we rooting our identity in the Word of God to not hinge our worth on words from others? Are we praying for a fresh perspective to allow God to work through our offended hearts and show us the state of someone else's need for the grace of Jesus in their lives?

The enemy wants to keep us chained in offense because it brings strife, discontent, anger, and self-righteousness – all things that take the focus off God and honor the enemy instead. He wants us to be in a stronghold of getting upset over others' words because it leaves less room for the TRUTH of God's word! He wants us to think about wounds, He wants us to talk about those wounds with others because that stirs up strife in their hearts too.

When someone gives you a dirty look when someone says something questionable, when someone says something stupid, when someone says something that is a LIE, when your character is questioned, when the character of those you love is questioned, when you are insecure, when you are hurt, when you are vulnerable....

God wants us to have VICTORY over these moments so we can WALK THE WALK of being a disciple of the Holy Spirit and the true power of the cross. That power can change our words, hearts, minds, and actions to bring honor TO HIM!

Has God used this study to change your perspective over the last six weeks?

_____

_____

_____

Journal Moment

Where has the Holy Spirit been convicting you of areas of growth through this Bible study?

_____

_____

_____

How has God used this study to change your perspective?

_____

_____

_____

How are you committed to putting what you've learned through this study into life application?

_____
_____
_____
_____
_____
_____
_____
_____
_____
_____
_____
_____
_____
_____
_____
_____
_____
_____
_____
_____
_____
_____

May this be our forever prayer: "Lord, shut my mouth and search my heart."

GROUP DISCUSSION QUESTIONS

Suggested format:

Each week that you meet together, discuss the book study in detail, watch the short video, and then work through these discussion questions.

Be open and vulnerable in sharing what God's stirring in your heart and discuss how to apply the learned content to your daily life.

Week 1

Are you easily angered by people's opinions or comments?

....

....

....

Do you tend to hold on to things people say or easily let it go?

....

....

....

How often do you engage on public social media posts with strangers? Do you find yourself getting upset with them?

Read 1 Corinthians 3:3

....

....

....

What are some examples of being "fleshly"?

....

....

....

Where is there strife in your relationships right now?

Read Colossians 3:12-17

....

....

....

What does verse 12 say that we are?

_____

_____

_____

What are we supposed to "put on", as Christ followers?

_____

_____

Why do you think he says we should "put them on"?

_____

_____

_____

Are you allowing peace to rule in your heart, over relationships, or are you allowing relationships to disrupt your peace? Discuss.

What does verse 16 say that we should do, to help how we interact with others?

_____

_____

_____

Do you notice a difference in how you interact with people if you've spent time studying God's word? Explain.

What are you hoping to learn through this study?

_____

_____

_____

Week 2

Read John 15 1-11

Based on this week's study, how can you apply this passage of scripture to your "roots"?

What are you rooted in right now that might be causing strain in relationships?

Who should we rely on to tend to our roots and fruit?

What does verse 4 call us to do?

How is your soil? How's your fruit?

Is the fruit of the spirit evident in your relationships?

Read John 15:12

Why is it so challenging to love other people?

How does this verse change our perspective on God's call to love others?

Read Ephesians 1:1-14

What does this passage say that we are, in Christ?

How does this passage help with working through some of our root issues? Discuss examples.

_____

_____

_____

Week 3

Read John 9:1-5

Do you tend to blame others when things go wrong?

_____

_____

_____

Do you get annoyed easily when things are inconvenient?

_____

_____

_____

Are there scenarios, or interactions that God is positioning you in, so that the works of him might be displayed in you?

_____

_____

_____

And if so, are you obeying the call and fulfilling your purpose in it?

_____

_____

_____

What situations are you facing this week that could use a "light of the world" perspective?

_____

_____

_____

Week 4

Have you ever "word-vomited" when you're stressed out?

_____

_____

_____

When you're in conversations with others, do you feel like you overshare with unfiltered words, or do you hold it in?

_____

_____

_____

Do you allow reflection time before responding in disagreements with people or do you react quickly?

Read Ephesians 4:1-3

_____

_____

_____

How does God call us to walk?

_____

_____

_____

How does this passage help our perspective in practicing the pause and choosing how we respond to people?

....

....

....

Week 5

Read Proverbs 14:29-30a

Are you more of a slow-to-anger or quick-to-anger person?

Read Proverbs 4:23

....

....

....

How do we guard our hearts?

Read Proverbs 15:4

....

....

....

What does this verse mean?

....

....

....

Have you ever known anyone that is good at calming people down?

Read Proverbs 18:4-8

....

....

....

Discuss the meaning of this passage.

....

....

....

How can we apply this to our interactions with people?

....

....

....

Week 6

Are you a "should have" or "would have" kind of person?

Where do you struggle with releasing control in relationships?

Do you find yourself having high expectations of others?

Do you offer advice to others without expectations of their actions in return? What are some examples of this?

Read 1 Thessalonians 4:4

One commentary on this verse says, "those who are busy bodies, meddling in other men's matters, have little quiet in their own minds and cause great disturbances."

Discuss what this means.

1 Thessalonians 4:11

_____

_____

_____

How does this verse guide us in creating healthy expectations and boundaries with others?

_____

_____

_____

Week 7

Read 2 Timothy 2: 1-4

What are we to be strong in?

_____

_____

_____

Read 2 Timothy 2:7-17

How does this passage encourage us in our perspectives and interactions with others?

_____

_____

_____

How has God spoken to you through this Bible study?

_____

_____

_____

What will you take from this study for life application?

_____

_____

_____

How will you use what you've studied over the last 6 weeks, to challenge and encourage yourself to walk in a manner worthy of your calling?

ACKNOWLEDGMENTS

To my husband, thank you for always cheering me on, believing in me, and encouraging me to do big things. I love you.

To my mentor and dear friend, Mary, thank you for saying yes. Thank you for walking with me hand in hand through all the seasons, with your wisdom and grace. I want to be just like you when I grow up.

To my coach, Alli, thank you for pushing me, holding me accountable, and supporting God's call on my life.

Xoxo,

Megan